Master Maths at Home

Whole Number Operations

Scan the QR code to help your child's learning at home.

MATHS
NO PROBLEM!

mastermathsathome.com

How to use this book

Maths — No Problem! created **Master Maths at Home** to help children develop fluency in the subject and a rich understanding of core concepts.

Key features of the Master Maths at Home books include:

- Carefully designed lessons that provide structure, but also allow flexibility in how they're used.

- Speech bubbles containing content designed to spark diverse conversations, with many discussion points that don't have obvious 'right' or 'wrong' answers.

- Rich illustrations that will guide children to a discussion of shapes and units of measurement, allowing them to make connections to the wider world around them.

- Exercises that allow a flexible approach and can be adapted to suit any child's cognitive or functional ability.

- Clearly laid-out pages that encourage children to practise a range of higher-order skills.

- A community of friendly and relatable characters who introduce each lesson and come along as your child progresses through the series.

You can see more guidance on how to use these books at **mastermathsathome.com**.

We're excited to share all the ways you can learn maths!

Copyright © 2022 Maths — No Problem!

Maths — No Problem!
mastermathsathome.com
www.mathsnoproblem.com
hello@mathsnoproblem.com

First published in Great Britain in 2022 by
Dorling Kindersley Limited
One Embassy Gardens, 8 Viaduct Gardens, London SW11 7BW
A Penguin Random House Company

The authorised representative in the EEA is Dorling Kindersley
Verlag GmbH. Arnulfstr. 124, 80636 Munich, Germany

10 9 8 7 6 5 4 3 2 1
001–327107–May/22

A CIP catalogue record for this book is available from the British Library.

ISBN: 978-0-24153-951-4
Printed and bound in the UK

For the curious
www.dk.com

MIX
Paper from
responsible sources
FSC™ C018179

This book was made with Forest Stewardship Council™ certified paper - one small step in DK's commitment to a sustainable future. For more information go to www.dk.com/our-green-pledge

Acknowledgements
The publisher would like to thank the authors and consultants Andy Psarianos, Judy Hornigold, Adam Gifford and Dr Anne Hermanson.

The Castledown typeface has been used with permission from the Colophon Foundry.

Contents

Ruby   Elliott   Amira   Charles   Lulu   Sam   Oak   Holly   Ravi   Emma   Jacob   Hannah

Order of operations (part 1)

Starter

Ruby and Sam are working on the same equation.

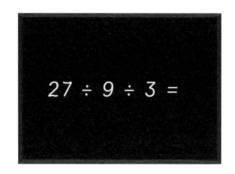

27 ÷ 9 ÷ 3 =

27 ÷ 9 ÷ 3 = 1

27 ÷ 9 ÷ 3 = 9

Whose answer is correct?

Example

Ruby started with 27 ÷ 9.

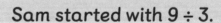

Sam started with 9 ÷ 3.

$27 \div 9 \div 3 = 3 \div 3$
$= 1$

$27 \div 9 \div 3 = 27 \div 3$
$= 9$

When we **divide**, we must work from left to right.

$27 \div 9 \div 3 = 1$
Ruby's answer is correct.

We must start with $27 \div 9$.

Try the following addition.

$4 + 6 + 3 = 10 + 3$
$= 13$

$4 + 6 + 3 = 4 + 9$
$= 13$

$4 + 6 + 3 = 7 + 6$
$= 13$

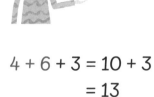

The order in which we **add** the numbers does not change the total.

Try the following multiplication.

$2 \times 3 \times 4 = 6 \times 4$
$= 24$

$2 \times 3 \times 4 = 2 \times 12$
$= 24$

$2 \times 3 \times 4 = 8 \times 3$
$= 24$

The order in which we multiply the numbers does not change the product.

Try the following subtraction.

$20 - 8 - 2 = 12 - 2$
$= 10$

$20 - 8 - 2 = 20 - 6$
$= 14$

In this example, $20 - 8 - 2$, we start by subtracting 8 from 20.

The order in which we subtract changes the difference. We must subtract from left to right.

1 Add.

(a) $12 + 6 + 8 =$ ⬚

(b) $45 + 11 + 20 =$ ⬚

2 Multiply.

(a) $4 \times 5 \times 3 =$ ⬚

(b) $2 \times 9 \times 5 =$ ⬚

3 Subtract.

(a) $43 - 7 - 5 =$ ⬚

(b) $62 - 12 - 9 =$ ⬚

(c) $105 - 25 - 19 =$ ⬚

(d) $234 - 121 - 5 =$ ⬚

4 Divide.

(a) $12 \div 3 \div 2 =$ ⬚

(b) $36 \div 12 \div 3 =$ ⬚

(c) $80 \div 20 \div 4 =$ ⬚

(d) $160 \div 8 \div 10 =$ ⬚

Order of operations (part 2)

Starter

Holly is working on this equation as part of her maths homework. Where should she start?

Example

32 ÷ (6 + 2)

This is called an expression.

There is an order when we work with expressions.

This is the order to follow.

1. Calculate the operations in the brackets.

2. Calculate operations that include numbers with indices.

Indices are the small numbers we sometimes find next to numbers, such as square numbers, 4^2, and cube numbers, 4^3.

3. Multiply and divide, in the order they are written, from left to right.

4. Add and subtract, in the order they are written, from left to right.

$32 \div (6 + 2) =$ [ ]

Start with the brackets.

$6 + 2 = 8$

$32 \div (6 + 2) = 32 \div 8$

$32 \div (6 + 2) = 32 \div 8$
$ = 4$

 Next, we divide.

$32 \div 8 = 4$

$32 \div (6 + 2) = 4$

Help Holly find the value of this expression.

$(46 + 14) \div 6 + 4 = \; ?$

Start with the brackets.

$(46 + 14) \div 6 + 4 = 60 \div 6 + 4$

Division is done before addition.

$$(46 + 14) \div 6 + 4 = 60 \div 6 + 4$$
$$= 10 + 4$$
$$= 14$$

1 Fill in the blanks.

(a) $(23 + 13) - 4 =$ ☐

(b) $12 + (45 + 8) - 7 =$ ☐

(c) $(4 \times 5) + (3 \times 2) =$ ☐

(d) $(58 + 14) \div 9 - 6 =$ ☐

2 Use brackets ( ) to give each equation a value of 45.

(a) $9 \times 4 + 1 = 45$

(b) $67 - 11 \times 2 = 45$

(c) $4 \times 5 + 5 \times 5 = 45$

(d) $75 \div 5 \times 3 = 45$

3 Use brackets ( ) to give each equation a different value.

(a) $14 + 5 \times 3 + 3 \times 2 =$ ☐

(b) $14 + 5 \times 3 + 3 \times 2 =$ ☐

(c) $14 + 5 \times 3 + 3 \times 2 =$ ☐

2-digit multiplication (part 1)

Starter

Sam's mum uses 231 g of flour to make a small loaf of bread. What is the total mass of flour that Sam's mum will need if she makes 20 small loaves of bread?

Example

Start by multiplying 231 by 10.

× 10

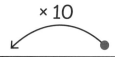

millions	hundred thousands	ten thousands	thousands	hundreds	tens	ones
				2	3	1
			2	3	1	0

231 × 1 ten = 231 tens
= 2310

Multiply 231 by 20.

231×2 tens $= 462$ tens
$= 4620$

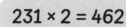
$231 \times 2 = 462$

If I know $231 \times 10 = 2310$, I can double the product.

$231 \times 10 = 2310$
$231 \times 20 = 4620$

$2310 + 2310 = 4620$

I know $231 \times 20 = 231 \times 2 \times 10$.

$231 \times 20 = 231 \times 2 \times 10$
$= 462 \times 10$
$= 4620$

Sam's mum will need 4620 g of flour to make 20 small loaves of bread.

What is 3231 × 20?

$3231 × 20 = 3231 × 2 × 10$
$ = 6462 × 10$
$ = 64\,620$

$3231 × 10 = 32\,310$
$3231 × 20 = 64\,620$

$32\,310 × 2 = 64\,620$

Practice

Multiply.

1   (a) $442 × 10 =$ ☐

      (b) $122 × 10 =$ ☐

      (c) $845 × 10 =$ ☐

      (d) $609 × 10 =$ ☐

2   (a)   331 × 10 = ☐   (b)   412 × 10 = ☐

                331 × 20 = ☐   412 × 20 = ☐

     (c)   312 × 10 = ☐   (d)   324 × 10 = ☐

                312 × 20 = ☐   324 × 20 = ☐

3   (a)   412 × 20 = 412 × 2 × 10

            = ☐

     (b)   323 × 30 = 323 × ☐ × ☐

            = ☐

4   A factory places 10 red pencil sharpeners and 10 blue pencil sharpeners into a single packet. 756 packets are placed into a large box.
How many pencil sharpeners are in the large box?

☐

There are pencil sharpeners in the large box.

2-digit multiplication (part 2)

Starter

Miss A'liya cut embroidery thread into lengths of 212 cm for her class.

If she gave a length of thread to each of the 22 pupils in her class, what was the total length of embroidery thread Miss A'liya used?

Example

22 = 20 + 2

Start by multiplying 212 by 2.

212 × 2 = 424

Multiply 212 by 20.

212 × 2 tens = 424 tens

424 tens = 4240

212 × 20 = 4240

212 × 2 = 424

212 × 22 = 4664

Miss A'liya used a total of 4664 cm of embroidery thread.

We can also use column multiplication.

Start by multiplying the ones.

```
      2  1  2
   ×     2  2
   ───────────
      4  2  4
 +
   ───────────
```

Next, multiply by the tens.

```
         2  1  2
   ×        2  2
   ───────────────
         4  2  4
 +  4  2  4  0
   ───────────────
    4  6  6  4
```

1 Multiply.

(a) 221 × 10 = ⬚

221 × 20 = ⬚

(b) 113 × 10 = ⬚

113 × 30 = ⬚

2 Find the product.

(a) 332 × 10 = ⬚

332 × 3 = ⬚

332 × 13 = ⬚

(b) 211 × 2 = ⬚

211 × 20 = ⬚

211 × 22 = ⬚

3 Multiply.

(a)
```
        2   3   3
  ×         1   2
  ─────────────────
      ⬚   ⬚   ⬚
+ ⬚   ⬚   ⬚   ⬚
  ─────────────────
  ⬚   ⬚   ⬚   ⬚
```

(b)
```
        1   2   2
  ×         3   1
  ─────────────────
      ⬚   ⬚   ⬚
+ ⬚   ⬚   ⬚   ⬚
  ─────────────────
  ⬚   ⬚   ⬚   ⬚
```

4 Every day in August, the maximum number of people rode the Cliff Edge rollercoaster.

If 213 is the maximum number of people the Cliff Edge rollercoaster can take in 1 day, how many people in total rode it during the month of August?

```
      2   1   3
  ×       3   1
  ┌───┬───┬───┐
  │   │   │   │
  └───┴───┴───┘
┌───┬───┬───┬───┐
│   │   │   │   │
+└───┴───┴───┴───┘
┌───┬───┬───┬───┐
│   │   │   │   │
└───┴───┴───┴───┘
```

┌─────────┐
│   │ people rode the Cliff Edge rollercoaster during the month
└─────────┘

of August.

5 In an office, 31 workers are given lunch every day that the office is open. If the office was open for 332 days in a single year, how many lunches were given to workers that year?

┌───┐
│   │
│   │
│   │
│   │
│   │
└───┘

There were ┌─────────┐ lunches given to workers that year.
           └─────────┘

2-digit multiplication (part 3)

Starter

Over the weekend, a supermarket sold 635 bags of bread rolls.
Each bag contained 2 dozen bread rolls.
What was the total number of bread rolls the supermarket sold over the weekend?

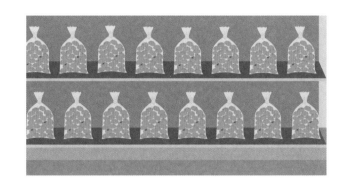

Example

Multiply 635 by 24.

2 dozen = 24

24 = 20 + 4

635 × 2 tens
= 1270 tens

$$\begin{array}{r} {}^{1}6\;{}^{2}3\;\;5 \\ \times \qquad\; 4 \\ \hline 2\;\;5\;\;4\;\;0 \\ \hline \end{array}$$

$$\begin{array}{r} 6\;{}^{1}3\;\;5 \\ \times \qquad 2\;\;0 \\ \hline 1\;\;2\;\;7\;\;0\;\;0 \\ \hline \end{array}$$

```
        6   3   5
×           2   4
─────────────────
    2   5   4   0      ⟶   635 × 4 = 2540
+ 1 2   7   0   0      ⟶   635 × 20 = 12 700
─────────────────
  1 5   2   4   0
─────────────────
```

Complete 635 × 24 using the column method.

Start by multiplying the ones.

```
        ¹6  ²3   5
×           2    4
─────────────────
    2   5   4    0
+
─────────────────
─────────────────
```

5 × 4 = 20

30 × 4 = 120
120 + 20 = 140

600 × 4 = 2400
2400 + 100 = 2500

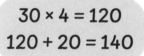
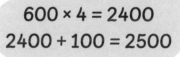

Multiply the tens.

```
        ¹6  ¹²3   5
×            2    4
──────────────────
    2    5   4    0
+ 1 2    7   0    0
──────────────────
  1 5    2   4    0
──────────────────
```

635 × 2 = 1270

635 × 24 = 15 240

The supermarket sold a total of 15 240 bread rolls over the weekend.

Practice

1 Multiply.

(a)

```
        4   3   6
    ×       1   2
    ┌───┬───┬───┐
    │   │   │   │
    └───┴───┴───┘
  ┌───┬───┬───┬───┐
+ │   │   │   │   │
  └───┴───┴───┴───┘
  ┌───┬───┬───┬───┐
  │   │   │   │   │
  └───┴───┴───┴───┘
```

(b)

```
        5   7   4
    ×       2   3
    ┌───┬───┬───┬───┐
    │   │   │   │   │
    └───┴───┴───┴───┘
  ┌───┬───┬───┬───┬───┐
+ │   │   │   │   │   │
  └───┴───┴───┴───┴───┘
  ┌───┬───┬───┬───┬───┐
  │   │   │   │   │   │
  └───┴───┴───┴───┴───┘
```

2 A North Atlantic right whale has a mass 84 times greater than a grey seal. If a grey seal has a mass of 268 kg, what is the mass of the North Atlantic right whale?

268 kg

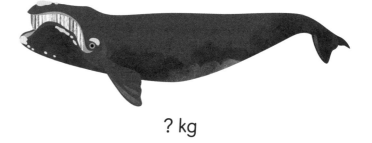

? kg

The North Atlantic right whale has a mass of ⬚ kg.

3 There are 36 eggs in a tray.
Every 6 months, a hotel uses 243 trays of eggs.
How may eggs does the hotel use in 6 months?

The hotel uses [   ] eggs in 6 months.

4 A baker uses 345 g of flour in every cake he makes.
If he makes 87 cakes in a week, what is the total mass of flour the baker uses in a week?

The baker uses [   ] g of flour in a week.

2-digit division (part 1)

Starter

A chef makes 390 samosas in 13 batches.
If the chef makes the same number of samosas
in each batch, how many samosas
does he make in a single batch?

Example

390 = 39 tens

39 is a multiple of 13.

$39 \div 3 = 13$
39 tens $\div$ 13 = 3 tens
$390 \div 13 = 30$

We can make 3 groups
of 13 from 39.

We can show this using
long division.

```
              3    0
   13 )   3   9    0
      -   3   9    0
      _____
                   0
```

39 tens $\div$ 13 = 3 tens

$390 \div 13 = 30$

The chef makes 30 samosas in a single batch.

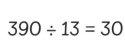

Practice

1 Divide.

(a) 24 ÷ 12 = ☐

240 ÷ 12 = ☐

2400 ÷ 12 = ☐

(b) 26 ÷ 13 = ☐

260 ÷ 13 = ☐

2600 ÷ 13 = ☐

(c) 480 ÷ 12 = ☐

4800 ÷ 12 = ☐

(d) 450 ÷ 15 = ☐

4500 ÷ 15 = ☐

2 (a)

```
        ☐ ☐
14 ) 2  8  0
   - ☐ ☐ ☐
   ─────────
           ☐
   ─────────
```

(b)

```
        ☐ ☐
12 ) 6  0  0
   - ☐ ☐ ☐
   ─────────
           ☐
   ─────────
```

3 A farm collects 720 eggs from their hens.
They put 12 eggs in each carton.
How many cartons can they fill with the eggs?

☐

The farm can fill ☐ cartons.

2-digit division (part 2)

Starter

A rollercoaster at an amusement park takes 26 people on each ride.
If 3224 people went on the rollercoaster in a single day, how many rides did it complete?

Example

Start by looking for multiples of 26.

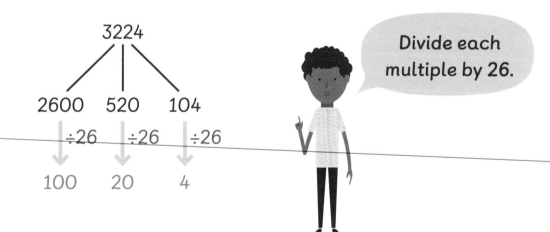

Divide each multiple by 26.

$3224 \div 26 = 124$

The rollercoaster completed 124 rides in a single day.

We can show this using long division.

```
              1
      ┌─────────────────
26  ) │   3   2   2   4
      │ - 2   6
      └─────────────────
              6   2   4
```

We can make 100 groups of 26 from 3200.

```
              1       2
      ┌─────────────────
26  ) │   3   2   2   4
      │ - 2   6
      └─────────────────
              6   2   4
      │ -     5   2
```

We can make 20 groups of 26 from 620.

```
              1   2   4
      ┌─────────────────
26  ) │   3   2   2   4
      │ - 2   6
      └─────────────────
              6   2   4
      │ -     5   2
      └─────────────────
                  1   0   4
      │ -         1   0   4
      └─────────────────
                          0
```

We can make 4 groups of 26 from 104.

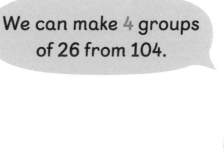

We can also show this using short division.

$$
\begin{array}{r}
1 \\
26 \overline{)\; 3 \diagup 2^{6} \;\; 2 \;\; 4}
\end{array}
$$

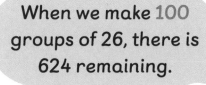

When we make 100 groups of 26, there is 624 remaining.

$$
\begin{array}{r}
1 \quad\; 2 \\
26 \overline{)\; 3 \diagup 2^{6\,1} \;\; 2^{0} \;\; 4}
\end{array}
$$

When we make 20 more groups of 26, there is 104 remaining.

$$
\begin{array}{r}
1 \quad\; 2 \quad\; 4 \\
26 \overline{)\; 3 \diagup 2^{6\,1} \;\; 2^{0} \;\; 4}
\end{array}
$$

When we make 4 more groups of 26, there is 0 remaining.

When 3224 is divided by 26, the quotient is 124.

3224 ÷ 26 = 124

Practice

1 Divide.

$2852 \div 23 =$ ⬚

$2300 \div 23 =$ ⬚

$460 \div 23 =$ ⬚

$92 \div 23 =$ ⬚

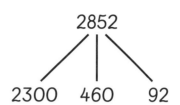

```
        2852
       / |  \
   2300  460  92
```

2 Use long division to find the quotient.

(a)

```
        ⬚ ⬚ ⬚
36 ) 4  0  6  8
   - ⬚ ⬚
   _____
     ⬚ ⬚ ⬚
   - ⬚ ⬚
   _____
     ⬚ ⬚ ⬚
   - ⬚ ⬚ ⬚
   _____
           ⬚
```

(b)

```
        ⬚ ⬚ ⬚
43 ) 5  2  8  9
   - ⬚ ⬚
   _____
     ⬚ ⬚ ⬚
   - ⬚ ⬚
   _____
     ⬚ ⬚ ⬚
   - ⬚ ⬚ ⬚
   _____
           ⬚
```

3 Use short division to find the quotient.

(a)
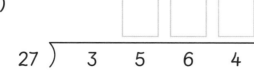

```
        ⬚ ⬚ ⬚
27 ) 3  5  6  4
```

(b)
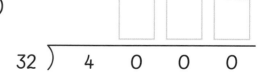

```
        ⬚ ⬚ ⬚
32 ) 4  0  0  0
```

2-digit division (part 3)

Starter

A water tank on a farm contains 3728 l of water. The farmer uses all the water in the tank to fill 32 containers with an equal amount of water.

What is the volume of water in each container?

Example

Use long division to divide 3728 by 32.

```
          1
32 )   3   7   2   8
     - 3   2
```

$3200 \div 32 = 100$

```
          1   1
32 )   3   7   2   8
     - 3   2
           5   2   8
         - 3   2
```

$320 \div 32 = 10$

```
          1    1    6
32 ) ‾‾‾3‾‾‾7‾‾‾2‾‾‾8‾‾
   −  3    2
   ‾‾‾‾‾‾‾‾‾‾‾‾‾‾‾‾‾‾‾‾‾
          5    2    8
   −       3    2
   ‾‾‾‾‾‾‾‾‾‾‾‾‾‾‾‾‾‾‾‾‾
          2    0    8
   −       1    9    2
   ‾‾‾‾‾‾‾‾‾‾‾‾‾‾‾‾‾‾‾‾‾
                    1    6
```

$192 \div 32 = 6$

We can show the remainder in different ways.

$3728 \div 32 = 116$ remainder 16

We can say there is a remainder of 16.

We can also show the remainder as a fraction or decimal.

We can simplify $\frac{16}{32}$.

$$3728 \div 32 = 116\frac{16}{32}$$
$$= 116\frac{1}{2}$$

The type of problem can help us decide how to show the remainder.

$3728 \div 32 = 116.5$

There is 116.5 l of water in each container.

Practice

1 Divide. Show the remainder as a decimal.

(a) 533 ÷ 26 = ☐

$$26 \overline{)\ 5\quad 3\quad 3}$$

r

(b) 7245 ÷ 36 = ☐

$$36 \overline{)\ 7\quad 2\quad 4\quad 5}$$

r

(c) 7242 ÷ 24 = ☐

$$24 \overline{)\ 7\quad 2\quad 4\quad 2}$$

r

(d) 9324 ÷ 45 = ☐

$$45 \overline{)\ 9\quad 3\quad 2\quad 4}$$

r

2 A juice bar uses 8424 ml of pineapple juice in 48 smoothies.
If they use the same amount of pineapple juice in each smoothie,
how many millilitres of pineapple juice is used in a single smoothie?

The juice bar uses [ ] ml of pineapple juice in a single smoothie.

3 3432 m of wire is cut into 96 equal lengths to use for fencing.
How long is each length of wire?

Each length of wire is [ ] m.

4 A factory has 1236 ml of perfume.
The perfume will be used to fill 48 ml bottles.
What is the maximum number of bottles the factory can fill?
What is the volume of perfume that will be left over?

The maximum number of bottles the factory can fill is [ ].

There will be [ ] ml of perfume left over.

Common multiples

Starter

There are 18 children who need to be put into teams of at least 3, with an equal number of children in each team.
How many different teams can be made?

Example

Can the children be put into teams of 3?
Find the multiples of 3.

3, 6, 9, 12, 15, 18

Find the multiples of 6.

6, 12, 18

Find the multiples of 9.

9, 18

18 is a multiple of 3, 6 and 9.

We say 18 is a **common multiple** of 3, 6 and 9.

18 children can be put into teams of 3, 6 and 9.

The smallest number of children we need to put into teams of 3, 6 and 9 is 18.

We say that 18 is the lowest common multiple of 3, 6 and 9.

Practice

1 Find 3 common multiples of the following numbers.

(a) 2 and 4 ☐ , ☐ , ☐

(b) 5 and 6 ☐ , ☐ , ☐

2 Find 3 common multiples of the following numbers.

(a) 2, 3 and 4 ☐ , ☐ , ☐

(b) 4, 5 and 10 ☐ , ☐ , ☐

3 Find the lowest common multiple of 10 and 12. ☐

Common factors

Starter

I think the numbers 14 and 21 have 2 common factors.

14   21

Is Emma correct?

Example

Start by finding the factors of each number.

Factors of 14: 1, 2, 7 and 14

$1 × 14 = 14$
$2 × 7 = 14$

Factors of 21: 1, 3, 7 and 21

$1 × 21 = 21$
$3 × 7 = 21$

All whole numbers have 1 as a factor.

7 is a common factor of 14 and 21.

The common factors of 14 and 21 are 1 and 7.

Emma is correct.

36

Find the common factors of 8, 12 and 20.

We know that 1 is a common factor of 8, 12 and 20.

All even numbers have a common factor of 2.

Factors of 8: 1, 2, 4 and 8
Factors of 12: 1, 2, 3, 4, 6 and 12
Factors of 20: 1, 2, 4, 5, 10 and 20

The common factors of 8, 12 and 20 are 1, 2 and 4.

The greatest common factor of 8, 12 and 20 is 4.

Practice

1 (a) Find the factors of 6: ☐ , ☐ , ☐ , ☐

Find the factors of 15: ☐ , ☐ , ☐ , ☐

The common factors of 6 and 15 are ☐ and ☐ .

(b) Find the factors of 27: ☐ , ☐ , ☐ , ☐

Find the factors of 24: ☐ , ☐ , ☐ , ☐ ,
☐ , ☐ , ☐ , ☐

The common factors of 27 and 24 are ☐ and ☐ .

2 Find the common factors of 18, 27 and 36.

☐ , ☐ , ☐

3 Find the greatest common factor of 24, 36 and 52. ☐

Prime numbers

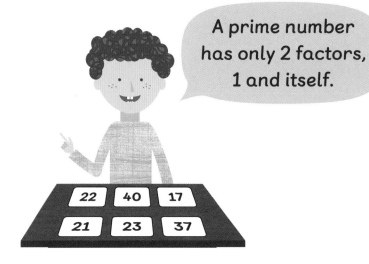

A prime number has only 2 factors, 1 and itself.

Which of the numbers on the table are prime numbers?

Example

All even numbers greater than 2 have 2 as a factor, as well as 1 and itself.

22 and 40 are not prime numbers.
They both have more than 2 factors.

The factors of 21 are 1, 3, 7 and 21.

21 is not a prime number. It has 4 factors.

21, 22 and 40 are composite numbers.

Composite numbers are whole numbers that have more than 2 factors.

The factors of 17 are 1 and 17.
The factors of 23 are 1 and 23.
The factors of 37 are 1 and 37.

17, 23 and 37 are prime numbers. The only factors each number has are 1 and itself.

Practice

1 Look at the following numbers and complete the sentences.

10   31   29   27   19   38   186   113

The composite numbers are _____.

The prime numbers are _____.

2 List the prime numbers between 50 and 70.

3 List the prime numbers between 80 and 100.

Review and challenge

1 Fill in the blanks.

(a) $4 \times 5 + 3 =$ ☐

(b) $10 + 27 \div 3 =$ ☐

(c) $(18 + 7) \div 5 + 2 =$ ☐

(d) $(3 + 7) + (4 \times 5) =$ ☐

2 Use brackets ( ) to give each equation a value of 32.

(a) $12 + 4 \times 5 = 32$

(b) $8 \times 16 \div 4 = 32$

(c) $27 + 40 - 15 + 20 = 32$

(d) $3 + 5 \times 5 - 1 = 32$

3 Multiply.

(a) $124 \times 10 =$ ☐

$124 \times 20 =$ ☐

(c) $153 \times 10 =$ ☐

$153 \times 20 =$ ☐

(b) $213 \times 10 =$ ☐

$213 \times 20 =$ ☐

(d) $321 \times 10 =$ ☐

$321 \times 30 =$ ☐

4 Multiply.

(a)
```
      2   1   2
  ×       4   1
  _____
  [ ] [ ] [ ]
[ ] [ ] [ ] [ ]
  _____
[ ] [ ] [ ] [ ]
  _____
```

(b)
```
      3   2   1
  ×       3   2
  _____
  [ ] [ ] [ ]
[ ] [ ] [ ] [ ]
  _____
[ ] [ ] [ ] [ ]
  _____
```

(c)
```
      4   3   4
  ×       5   5
  _____
  [ ] [ ] [ ] [ ]
[ ] [ ] [ ] [ ] [ ]
  _____
[ ] [ ] [ ] [ ] [ ]
  _____
```

(d)
```
      6   3   8
  ×       4   7
  _____
  [ ] [ ] [ ] [ ]
[ ] [ ] [ ] [ ] [ ]
  _____
[ ] [ ] [ ] [ ] [ ]
  _____
```

5 Divide.

(a) $48 \div 12 = $ [ ]

   $480 \div 12 = $ [ ]

(b) $39 \div 13 = $ [ ]

   $390 \div 13 = $ [ ]

(c) $960 \div 16 = $ [ ]

   $96 \div 16 = $ [ ]

(d) $840 \div 14 = $ [ ]

   $84 \div 14 = $ [ ]

6 Divide.

(a)

```
        ┌──┬──┬──┐
        │  │  │  │
   34 ) 5  8  8  2
      ┌──┬──┐
    - │  │  │
      └──┴──┘
      ┌──┬──┬──┐
      │  │  │  │
      │  │  │  │
    - │  │  │  │
      └──┴──┴──┘
        ┌──┬──┬──┐
        │  │  │  │
        │  │  │  │
      - │  │  │  │
        └──┴──┴──┘
           ┌──┐
           │  │
           └──┘
```

(b)

```
        ┌──┬──┬──┐    ┌──┬──┐
        │  │  │  │  r │  │  │
   48 ) 7  5  5  0    └──┴──┘
      ┌──┬──┐
    - │  │  │
      └──┴──┘
      ┌──┬──┬──┐
      │  │  │  │
      │  │  │  │
    - │  │  │  │
      └──┴──┴──┘
        ┌──┬──┬──┐
        │  │  │  │
        │  │  │  │
      - │  │  │  │
        └──┴──┴──┘
           ┌──┐
           │  │
           └──┘
```

7 Find 3 common multiples of 3, 4 and 6.

☐ , ☐ , ☐

8 Find the lowest common multiple of 8 and 12. ☐

9 Find the common factors of 21 and 35. ☐ , ☐

10 Find the greatest common factor of 14, 49 and 56. ☐

11 List the prime numbers between 30 and 50.

☐

12 Elliott's mum is making bagels. She needs to use 70 g of plain flour and 65 g of bread flour for each bagel.
If she makes 40 bagels, how many grams of flour will she use altogether?

Elliott's mum will use ☐ g of flour altogether.

13 A group of children are put into equal sized groups for an activity afternoon. The children are put into groups of either exactly 24 children or exactly 32 children.
What is the smallest possible number of children participating in the activity afternoon?

The smallest possible number of children participating in the activity afternoon is ☐ .

14 The 18th-century Russian mathematician Christian Goldbach made the famous conjecture (a conjecture is a best guess or opinion) that every even whole number greater than 2 is the sum of two prime numbers. Find the missing prime numbers.

(a) 4 = 2 + 2

1 is not a prime number.

(b) 16 = ☐ + ☐

(c) 10 = ☐ + ☐

(d) 18 = ☐ + ☐

(e) 50 = ☐ + ☐

(f) 98 = ☐ + ☐

15 A train makes a return journey between London and Birmingham 7 times a day. The train can hold 367 passengers. Last Monday, the train was full of different passengers for each leg of the journey. How many people in total travelled on the train last Monday?

Last Monday, ☐ passengers travelled on the train in total.

16 A factory produces 147 notepads each hour for 12 hours a day.
If the notepads are put into packets of 14, how many packets can be filled in 1 day?

The factory can fill [ ] packets in 1 day.

17 A new bakery made some cakes to deliver to a supermarket.
On Tuesday, they made twice as many cakes as they made on Monday.
On Wednesday, they made as many cakes as they made in total on Monday and Tuesday.

(a) If they made 94 cakes on Tuesday, how many cakes did the new bakery make over the 3 days?

The new bakery made [ ] cakes over the 3 days.

(b) If they used 28 chocolate decorations on each cake, how many chocolate decorations did the new bakery use over the 3 days?

The new bakery used [ ] chocolate decorations over the 3 days.

Answers

Page 7   **1 (a)** $12 + 6 + 8 = 26$ **(b)** $45 + 11 + 20 = 76$ **2 (a)** $4 \times 5 \times 3 = 60$ **(b)** $2 \times 9 \times 5 = 90$ **3 (a)** $43 - 7 - 5 = 31$
           (b) $62 - 12 - 9 = 41$ **(c)** $105 - 25 - 19 = 61$ **(d)** $234 - 121 - 5 = 108$ **4 (a)** $12 \div 3 \div 2 = 2$ **(b)** $36 \div 12 \div 3 = 1$
           (c) $80 \div 20 \div 4 = 1$ **(d)** $160 \div 8 \div 10 = 2$

Page 11   **1 (a)** $(23 + 13) - 4 = 32$ **(b)** $12 + (45 + 8) - 7 = 58$ **(c)** $(4 \times 5) + (3 \times 2) = 26$ **(d)** $(58 + 14) \div 9 - 6 = 2$
           2 (a) $9 \times (4 + 1) = 45$ **(b)** $67 - (11 \times 2) = 45$ **(c)** $(4 \times 5) + (5 \times 5) = 45$ **(d)** $(75 \div 5) \times 3 = 45$ **3 (a–c)** Answers will vary.
           For example: $(14 + 5) \times 3 + (3 \times 2) = 63$, $(14 + 5) \times (3 + 3) \times 2 = 228$, $14 + (5 \times 3) + (3 \times 2) = 35$

Page 14   **1 (a)** $442 \times 10 = 4420$ **(b)** $122 \times 10 = 1220$ **(c)** $845 \times 10 = 8450$ **(d)** $609 \times 10 = 6090$

Page 15   **2 (a)** $331 \times 10 = 3310$, $331 \times 20 = 6620$ **(b)** $412 \times 10 = 4120$, $412 \times 20 = 8240$ **(c)** $312 \times 10 = 3120$, $312 \times 20 = 6240$
           (d) $324 \times 10 = 3240$, $324 \times 20 = 6480$ **3 (a)** $412 \times 20 = 412 \times 2 \times 10 = 8240$ **(b)** $323 \times 30 = 323 \times 3 \times 10 = 9690$
           4 $756 \times 2 \times 10 = 15\,120$. There are 15 120 pencil sharpeners in the large box.

Page 18   **1 (a)** $221 \times 10 = 2210$, $221 \times 20 = 4420$ **(b)** $113 \times 10 = 1130$, $113 \times 30 = 3390$
           2 (a) $332 \times 10 = 3320$, $332 \times 3 = 996$, $332 \times 13 = 4316$ **(b)** $211 \times 2 = 422$, $211 \times 20 = 4220$, $211 \times 22 = 4642$

3 (a)
```
        2   3   3
  ×         1   2
  ─────────────────
        4   6   6
  +  2   3   3   0
  ─────────────────
     2   7   9   6
```

(b)
```
        1   2   2
  ×         3   1
  ─────────────────
        1   2   2
  +  3   6   6   0
  ─────────────────
     3   7   8   2
```

Page 19   **4**
```
        2   1   3
  ×         3   1
  ─────────────────
        2   1   3
  +  6  ¹3   9   0
  ─────────────────
     6   6   0   3
```
6603 people rode the Cliff Edge rollercoaster during the month of August.

5
```
        3   3   2
  ×         3   1
  ─────────────────
        3   3   2
  +    ¹9   9   6   0
  ─────────────────
     1   0   2   9   2
```
There were 10 292 lunches given to workers that year.

Page 22   **1 (a)**
```
        4  ¹3   6
  ×         1   2
  ─────────────────
       ¹8   7   2
  + ¹4   3   6   0
  ─────────────────
     5   2   3   2
```

(b)
```
       ¹2  5  ¹7   4
  ×             2   3
  ──────────────────────
       ¹1  ¹7   2   2
  +  1   1   4   8   0
  ──────────────────────
     1   3   2   0   2
```

2
```
       ⁵2  ⁶6   8
  ×             8   4
  ──────────────────────
       1  ¹0   7   2
  +  2   1   4   4   0
  ──────────────────────
     2   2   5   1   2
```
The North Atlantic right whale has a mass of 22 512 kg.

Page 23   **3**
```
       ²2  ¹4   3
  ×             3   6
  ──────────────────────
     1  ¹4   5   8
  +  7   2   9   0
  ──────────────────────
     8   7   4   8
```
The hotel uses 8748 eggs in 6 months.

4
```
       ³3  ⁴4   5
  ×             8   7
  ──────────────────────
       ¹2   4   1   5
  + ¹2   7   6   0   0
  ──────────────────────
     3   0   0   1   5
```
The baker uses 30 015 g of flour in a week.

Page 25 **1 (a)** $24 \div 12 = 2$, $240 \div 12 = 20$, $2400 \div 12 = 200$ **(b)** $26 \div 13 = 2$, $260 \div 13 = 20$, $2600 \div 13 = 200$
(c) $480 \div 12 = 40$, $4800 \div 12 = 400$ **(d)** $450 \div 15 = 30$, $4500 \div 15 = 300$

2 (a)
```
            2  0
  14 ) 2  8  0
     - 2  8  0
             0
```
(b)
```
            5  0  3
  12 ) 6  0  0
     - 6  0  0
             0
```
```
            6  0
  12 ) 7  2  0
     - 7  2  0
             0
```
The farm can fill 60 cartons.

Page 29 **1** $2852 \div 23 = 124$, $2300 \div 23 = 100$, $460 \div 23 = 20$, $92 \div 23 = 4$

2 (a)
```
            1  1  3
  36 ) 4  0  6  8
     - 3  6
        4  6  8
     -  3  6
        1  0  8
     -  1  0  8
              0
```
(b)
```
            1  2  3
  43 ) 5  2  8  9
     - 4  3
        9  8  9
     -  8  6
        1  2  9
     -  1  2  9
              0
```
3 (a)
```
            1  3  2
  27 ) 3  5  ⁸6  ⁵4
```
(b)
```
            1  2  5
  32 ) 4  0  ⁸0  ¹⁶0
```

Page 32 **1 (a)** $533 \div 26 = 20.5$
```
            2  0  r 13
  26 ) 5  3  3
     - 5  2
        1  3
```
(b) $7245 \div 36 = 201.25$
```
            2  0  1  r 9
  36 ) 7  2  4  5
     - 7  2
           4  5
        -  3  6
              9
```

(c) $7242 \div 24 = 301.75$
```
            3  0  1  r 18
  24 ) 7  2  4  2
     - 7  2
           4  2
        -  2  4
           1  8
```
(d) $9324 \div 45 = 207.2$
```
            2  0  7  r 9
  45 ) 9  3  2  4
     - 9  0
           3  2  4
        -  3  1  5
              9
```

Page 33 **2**
```
            1  7  5  r 24
  48 ) 8  4  2  4
     - 4  8
        3  6  2  4
     -  3  3  6  0
           2  6  4
        -  2  4  0
              2  4
```
The juice bar uses 175.5 OR $175\frac{1}{2}$ ml of pineapple juice in a single smoothie.

3
```
            3  5  r 72
  96 ) 3  4  3  2
     - 2  8  8
        5  5  2
     -  4  8  0
           7  2
```
Each length of wire is 35.75 OR $35\frac{3}{4}$ m.

4
```
            2  5  r 36
  48 ) 1  2  3  6
     -  9  6
        2  7  6
     -  2  4  0
           3  6
```
The maximum number of bottles the factory can fill is 25.
There will be 36 ml of perfume left over.

Page 35 **1** Answers will vary. For example: **(a)** 8, 12, 16 **(b)** 30, 60, 90 **2** Answers will vary. For example: **(a)** 12, 24, 36 **(b)** 20, 40, 60 **3** 60

Page 37 **1 (a)** 1, 2, 3, 6; 1, 3, 5, 15. The common factors of 6 and 15 are 1 and 3. **(b)** 1, 3, 9, 27; 1, 2, 3, 4, 6, 8, 12, 24. The common factors of 27 and 24 are 1 and 3. **2** 1, 3, 9 **3** 4

Page 39 **1** The composite numbers are 10, 27, 38 and 186. The prime numbers are 31, 29, 19 and 113. **2** 53, 59, 61, 67. **3** 83, 89, 97

Page 40 **1 (a)** $4 \times 5 + 3 = 23$ **(b)** $10 + 27 \div 3 = 19$ **(c)** $(18 + 7) \div 5 + 2 = 7$ **(d)** $(3 + 7) + (4 \times 5) = 30$ **2 (a)** $12 + (4 \times 5) = 32$
(b) $8 \times (16 \div 4) = 32$ **(c)** $27 + 40 - (15 + 20) = 32$ **(d)** $(3 + 5) \times (5 - 1) = 32$ **3 (a)** $124 \times 10 = 1240$, $124 \times 20 = 2480$
(b) $213 \times 10 = 2130$, $213 \times 20 = 4260$ **(c)** $153 \times 10 = 1530$, $153 \times 20 = 3060$ **(d)** $321 \times 10 = 3210$, $321 \times 30 = 9630$

Answers continued

Page 41 **4 (a)**

```
        2   1   2
    ×       4   1
  ─────────────────
        2   1   2
  + 8   4   8   0
  ─────────────────
    8   6   9   2
```

(b)

```
            3   2   1
    ×           3   2
  ─────────────────────
            6   4   2
  +   ¹9    6   3   0
  ─────────────────────
      1    0   2   7   2
```

(c)

```
          ¹4  ²3   4
    ×         5   5
  ─────────────────────
      2   1   7   0
  + 2  1   7   0   0
  ─────────────────────
    2  3   8   7   0
```

(d)

```
          ¹6  ³3   8
    ×         4   7
  ─────────────────────
      4   4   6   6
  + 2  5   5   2   0
  ─────────────────────
    2  9   9   8   6
```

5 (a) $48 \div 12 = 4$, $480 \div 12 = 40$ **(b)** $39 \div 13 = 3$, $390 \div 13 = 30$ **(c)** $960 \div 16 = 60$, $96 \div 16 = 6$
(d) $840 \div 14 = 60$, $84 \div 14 = 6$

Page 42 **6 (a)**

```
              1   7   3
      34 ) 5  8   8   2
         - 3  4
         ─────────
           2  4   8
         - 2  3   8
         ─────────
              1  0   2
         -    1  0   2
         ─────────
                     0
```

(b)

```
              1   5   7  r 14
      48 ) 7  5   5   0
         - 4  8
         ─────────
           2  7   5
         - 2  4   0
         ─────────
           3  5   0
         - 3  3   6
         ─────────
                 1   4
```

7 Answers will vary: For example: 12, 24, 36
8 24 **9** 1, 7 **10** 7 **11** 31, 37, 41, 43, 47

Page 43 **12**

```
        ¹1  ²3   5
    ×       4   0
  ─────────────────
    5   4   4   0
```

Elliott's mum will use 5400 g of flour altogether.

13 24, 48, 72, 96; 32, 64, 96. The smallest possible number of children participating in the activity afternoon is 96.

Page 44 **14 (b)** 16 = 11 + 5 OR 16 = 3 + 13 **(c)** 10 = 5 + 5 OR 10 = 3 + 7 **(d)** 18 = 11 + 7 OR 18 = 5 + 13
(e) 50 = 13 + 37, 50 = 43 + 7, 50 = 47 + 3 OR 50 = 31 + 19 **(f)** 98 = 67 + 31, 98 = 19 + 79 OR 98 = 37 + 61

15

```
        ²3  ²6   7
    ×       1   4
  ─────────────────
    ¹1 ¹4   6   8
  + 3   6   7   0
  ─────────────────
    5   1   3   8
```

Last Monday, 5138 passengers travelled on the train in total.

Page 45 **16**

```
        1  ¹4   7
    ×      1   2
  ─────────────────
       ¹2  9   4
  + 1   4   7   0
  ─────────────────
    1   7   6   4
```

```
              1   2   6
      14 ) 1  7   6   4
         - 1  4
         ─────────
           3  6
         - 2  8
         ─────────
              8   4
         -    8   4
         ─────────
                     0
```

The factory can fill 126 packets in 1 day.

17 (a) Monday = $94 \div 2 = 47$; Tuesday = 94; Wednesday = $47 + 94 = 141$; $47 + 94 + 141 = 282$. The new bakery made 282 cakes over the 3 days.

(b)

```
        ¹6  ²8   2
    ×       2   8
  ─────────────────
    2   2   5   6
  + 5   6   4   0
  ─────────────────
    7   8   9   6
```

The new bakery used 7896 chocolate decorations over the 3 days.